Creative Education

BY VALERIE BODDEN

Published by Creative Education
P.O. Box 227, Mankato, Minnesota 56002
Creative Education is an imprint of The Creative Company
www.thecreativecompany.us

Cover design and art direction by Rita Marshall
Interior design and book production by The Design Lab
Printed in the United States of America

Photographs by Alamy (ClassicStock, Classic Image,
Hipix, INTERFOTO Pressebildagentur, North Wind Picture
Archives, Stock Montage, Inc., The London Art Archive),
Corbis (H. Armstrong Roberts, Bettmann, Brooklyn Museum,
Burstein Collection, Matthew Cavanagh/epa, Hulton-Deutsch
Collection), iStockphoto

Library of Congress Cataloging-in-Publication Data
Bodden, Valerie.
The Declaration of American Independence / by Valerie
Bodden.
p. cm. – (Days of change)
Includes bibliographical references and index.
ISBN 978-1-58341-733-1
1. United States–Declaration of Independence–Juvenile
literature. 2. United States–History–Colonial period, ca.
1600–1775–Juvenile literature. 3. United States–History–
Revolution, 1775–1783–Juvenile literature. 4. United States–
Politics and government–1775–1783–Juvenile literature. I.
Title. II. Series.
E221.B64 2009
973.3'13–dc22   2008009164

First Edition
9 8 7 6 5 4 3 2 1

THE DECLARATION OF AMERICAN INDEPENDENCE

In one of the first demonstrative acts of the American Revolution, colonists tore dow

Hundreds of people packed the courtyard

of the State House in Philadelphia, Pennsylvania, on Monday, July 8, 1776. Sweating in the noontime sun, the crowds listened carefully as Colonel John Nixon of the Philadelphia Committee of Safety read: "When in the Course of human events, it becomes necessary for one people to dissolve the political bands which have connected them with another, . . ." When he reached the conclusion, that "these United Colonies are, and of Right ought to be Free and Independent States," the crowd broke into cheers. Several men pulled down the coat of arms of the British king from an inner wall of the State House. This shield-shaped emblem symbolizing British authority was no longer needed. The American colonies had declared their independence.

America wasn't free from British rule yet, though. In the years following its bold declaration, the self-proclaimed United States of America still had to win its freedom from Britain through the bloody Revolutionary War. When it finally did so, the Declaration of Independence became a beacon of hope to nations around the world, moving many to fight for their own independence. Indeed, still today, the American Declaration of Independence inspires nations and individuals to seek its promises of "life, liberty, and the pursuit of happiness."

5

The Declaration of Independence was penned during a period in the Western world (the part of the world including Europe and America) known as the Age of Enlightenment. People of this time were amazed by the scientific discoveries of the previous century, including Isaac Newton's theory that a force called gravity pulls objects toward one another. They believed that they were living in an "age of light," during which not only the laws of the universe but also the laws of human society could be discovered. Enlightened philosophers such as Voltaire of France and Immanuel Kant of Germany turned from the strong focus on religion that had marked previous centuries to a focus on reason as a means of achieving progress.

AN ENLIGHTENED WORLD

The Enlightenment was centered largely in France, where writers known as *philosophes* turned out numerous works about government, religion, and freedom. Their works had little effect on the government of their own country, however, as both King Louis XV and his successor, King Louis XVI, were wasteful and repressive and cared little about improving the lives of their subjects. Enlightenment thought did have an effect on the rulers of other nations, though. Especially in Prussia (a former kingdom of Germany), Russia, and Austria, rulers known as enlightened despots sought to retain power by initiating significant reforms such as religious tolerance, improvements in living conditions, and wider access to education.

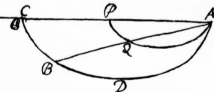

Even with such reforms, enlightened despots still held absolute control over their countries. The same was not true in Britain. Although King George III still wielded considerable power, Parliament had the authority to pass laws and impose taxes on the 15 million subjects of the British Empire, which stretched around the world. In England, the seat of the empire, the Industrial Revolution took hold in the late 1700s. This period of rapid development in manufacturing techniques led to the establishment of factories in cities across the country. People were soon relocating to these cities in search of new job opportunities, and by the latter half of the century, London was one of the largest cities in the world, with a population nearing one million.

Even while overseeing such progress at home, Britain, along with Spain and Portugal, ruled over a number of colonies on the other side of the world, in the Americas. Abundant natural resources and huge farms known as plantations made these colonies a source of wealth for the European nations that ruled them. But in order to extract this wealth from the land, huge numbers of laborers were needed. These laborers were provided through the slave trade, in which European merchants purchased men, women, and children from Africa, then shipped them across the Atlantic to the Americas.

"Everything we believe in as Americans . . . our noblest ideas, our highest aspirations, all came out of the Revolution. Equality, liberty, Constitutionalism, the well-being of ordinary people, self-government—all of these things came out of the Revolution. That is why we go down to [America's] founding to reaffirm [the] values that held us together. To be an American is not to be somebody, but to believe in something."

Dr. Gordon S. Wood,
American historian, 2007

8

Much of the early economic success in colonies in the Americas was built on the backs of slaves, who were most often captured in West Africa and shipped across the Atlantic Ocean.

"*The true soul of the Declaration of Independence lies . . . in the middle portion's mundane bill of particulars. By listing in exhaustive detail the depredations [attacks] of King George III and stressing the patience with which the colonists had borne them, the Congress hoped to discourage other rebels from acting too precipitately [quickly]. Unfortunately, . . . the catalogue of injustices has been all too easy to ignore. . . . The result . . . has been that revolutionaries . . . have tried to overthrow governments without carefully weighing their grievances and exhausting their forbearance [patience].*"

FREDERIC SCHWARZ,
author for *American Heritage* magazine, 2001

The majority of the 80,000 or more African slaves brought to the New World every year ended up in South America. Most of this continent had been divided between Spain and Portugal in the 16th and 17th centuries. Although gold and silver mines and flourishing farms helped to enrich the Spanish and Portuguese colonies, there was also discontent among the colonists. Trade restrictions and taxes imposed by the mother countries cut into colonial profits. In addition, colonists who had been born to European parents in South America (called Creoles) were angered that they were kept from holding positions of power, which were reserved for those who had been born in Europe (called *peninsulares*).

11

Meanwhile, just as Spain and Portugal had a hold on South America, the British ruled 13 colonies farther north—on the eastern coast of North America. The first British colonists had arrived in America in 1607. There, they had established the first permanent English settlement at Jamestown, in Virginia. Since that time, thousands of people from Europe had set sail for America. Many sought religious freedom or an escape from war in their homeland. Others were in search of cheap land. By the 1770s, the 13 colonies that ran down the Atlantic seaboard from present-day Maine (then part of Massachusetts) to Georgia were home to 2.75 million people. In the south, powerful landowners ran huge plantations, on which they used slave

The slave trade was a convenient business for colonists; buyers awaited slave ships in ports, where the imprisoned Africans would be inspected and sold to the highest bidders.

laborers to grow cotton, rice, and tobacco. In the north, wealthy merchants conducted business in thriving cities such as Boston, Philadelphia, and New York.

Although the colonies were part of the British Empire, until the 1760s, the motherland left the colonists to govern themselves for the most part. While Britain regulated the colonies' trade and defense and appointed colonial governors, each colony also had its own legislature consisting of elected representatives. The legislature had the power to pass laws and levy taxes.

After Britain's 1763 victory in the French and Indian War, however, the empire was left with an enormous debt. Because this war had been fought against France and its American Indian allies for control of much of the North American continent, the British believed that the

The French and Indian War, which began in 1754, eventually reached all the way to Europe (where it was known as the Seven Years' War). The American theater of the war began over control of the Ohio River Valley, where the French had built a number of forts to protect their fur trade with the Native Americans, many of whom had been pushed off their land by the British. During the war, many American Indians aided the French, while the American colonists fought for Britain. After winning the war, the British took over all lands east of the Mississippi, including French-controlled Canada and Spanish-held Florida.

George Washington (on horseback) served Britain loyally during the French and Indian War and was given land in Virginia as a reward after helping the motherland earn victory.

Illustrations and engravings of the Boston Massacre, such as this one by famed colonial patriot Paul Revere, were used to help inflame anti-British sentiment among the colonies.

Colonial tax stamp

colonists had bene-fited most from the wartime victory. As a result, the British parliament began to tax the colonies to raise revenue. The Sugar Act of 1764 placed a tax on molasses and other luxuries imported to the colonies, while the Stamp Act of 1765 required the colonists to purchase tax stamps for all written documents. In response, the outraged colonists boycotted British goods, and angry mobs burned the houses of tax collectors.

As a result, Britain repealed the Stamp Act, only to replace it with the Townshend Acts of 1767, which taxed imported products such as paper, paint, lead, and tea. Again, the colonists initiated a boycott. Samuel Adams, a politician from Massachusetts, wrote a paper protesting taxation without representation (since the colonists were being taxed without being allowed to send a representative to the British parliament). In response, Britain dissolved the legislatures of Massachusetts and Virginia, both of which had supported the paper. The motherland also immediately dispatched troops for Boston in case the colonists should decide to rebel.

Britain's actions angered many colonists. On March 5, 1770, a crowd of about 400 men gathered outside a customs house in Boston and began to throw rocks and chunks of ice at eight British guards. In response, the guards opened fire, killing five colonists in what came to be known as the Boston Massacre. Afterward, Britain

15

repealed the Townshend Acts, except for the tax on tea, which was kept as a symbol of the Parliament's authority to tax the colonies. Then, in 1773, Britain passed the Tea Act, which kept the tax on tea but allowed the British East India Company to sell cheap tea in the colonies, undercutting local merchants. In protest, between 50 and 200 men from Boston disguised themselves as Indians and boarded three British ships in December, dumping 90,000 pounds (40,800 kg) of tea into the harbor.

The British response to the so-called Boston Tea Party was harsh. In 1774, Parliament passed a series of laws known in the colonies as the Intolerable Acts. These laws closed Boston's port and gave Britain control over the election of colonial officials. In response, on September 5, 1774, leaders from 12 of the 13 colonies met in Philadelphia at the First

In addition to opposing the taxes levied on the colonies by Britain, Americans were also angered by other British laws, including the Quartering Act of 1765. This act ordered the colonists to provide housing for British soldiers in American barracks, inns, stables, or other uninhabited buildings. The colonists were also forced to provide the soldiers with supplies, including salt, alcohol, and candles, sometimes free of charge. Many Americans resented this law, as it required them to pay to keep unwanted British troops in the colonies. In 1766, New York refused to house 1,500 British soldiers, and as a result, its legislature was suspended.

When British General Thomas Gage set out for Concord to confiscate American arms in April 1775, he thought his mission would be easy. Like other Britons, he thought Americans were undisciplined and cowardly. On the way to Concord, however, Gage and his 700 troops were met by 70 local militiamen in Lexington. When a firefight broke out, the colonists stood their ground even as eight Americans (and no redcoats) were killed. Colonial militiamen also fought the British in Concord, where two colonists and three redcoats were killed. And as the British marched back to Boston, the colonists shot at them along the road, killing another 70.

Continental Congress (an association that was illegal under British law). The Congress encouraged a continued boycott of British products and drafted a petition to King George III, seeking a peaceful resolution of their differences. At the same time, the Congress warned the colonists that the dispute with Britain might result in armed conflict.

They were right. In April 1775, some 700 British soldiers (called redcoats by the colonists because of their red uniforms) set out for Concord, a town 21 miles (34 km) northwest of Boston. Their mission was to seize weapons hidden there by the Americans. On their way, the British troops encountered local militiamen at Lexington, where a soldier—no one knows from which side—fired a shot, setting off the Revolutionary War. The long battle for freedom had begun.

The leaders of the American colonies reacted swiftly to the beginning of open warfare. On May 10, 1775, delegates representing all 13 colonies gathered at the State House in Philadelphia for the Second Continental Congress. Among the 69 delegates were many, such as Samuel Adams and John Adams of Massachusetts, who had attended the First Continental Congress. Others, including Thomas Jefferson of Virginia, Benjamin Franklin of Pennsylvania, and John Hancock of Massachusetts, were new to the Congress. Most of the delegates were among the wealthiest people in the colonies. Some were politicians by profession, while others were lawyers, physicians, merchants, or landowners.

THE PURSUIT OF INDEPENDENCE

The delegates elected Hancock, a wealthy merchant, as president of the Congress, and chose George Washington, an officer in Virginia's militia, to lead the new Continental Army, made up of volunteers from all the colonies. The congressional delegates also debated how best to end the conflict with Britain. Some were in favor of immediately cutting all ties with the British crown and declaring their independence. Others wanted to make peace with their motherland.

As a compromise, the delegates decided to make one more attempt at a diplomatic solution while also gearing up for continued warfare. In July 1775, the Congress sent King George III the Olive Branch Petition. This document stated that if England would address the colonists' complaints about the unfair taxes that had been imposed upon them, Americans would remain loyal to the Crown. When the king refused to so

20

The delegates arriving in Philadelphia for the 1776 meeting of the Second Continental Congress found themselves in the largest city in the American colonies. Located at the crossroads of the colonies, Philadelphia was a melting pot of people from across the world. Its 30,000 residents encompassed people of British, Dutch, German, Swedish, and African (most of whom were slaves) descent. Philadelphia was also one of the most progressive cities in America, with lighted, paved streets, a public library, and shops for the manufacture of everything from furniture to pocket watches. Taverns throughout the city served as places for residents to discuss politics, business, and news.

It was under the roof of Philadelphia's State House (later called Independence Hall) that both the American Declaration of Independence and the Constitution were drafted.

Virginian Richard Henry Lee

much as read the petition, the colonies stepped up their war preparation efforts. They built up their meager supply of weapons—such as muskets and cannons—and established a navy.

Just as the Congress was divided over the issue of independence, so too were the American colonists. Some, known as Whigs, or patriots, supported American independence. Others, known as Tories, or loyalists, remained faithful to England. Heated discussions took place in taverns across the colonies, and fiery speeches were delivered in churches and public squares, while pamphlets about the justness of the American cause flew off colonial presses. In January

1776, a 50-page pamphlet called *Common Sense* by radical philosopher Thomas Paine declared, "Every thing that is right or reasonable pleads for separation. The blood of the slain, the weeping voice of nature cries, 'TIS TIME TO PART." As nearly every family in America read or heard about the pamphlet, revolutionary fervor ignited the colonies.

In this atmosphere, Richard Henry Lee, a 44-year-old politician from Virginia, made a bold resolution on June 7, 1776: "That these United Colonies are, and of Right ought to be Free and Independent States; that they are Absolved from all Allegiance to the British Crown,

22

COMMON SENSE:

ADDRESSED TO THE

INHABITANTS

OF

AMERICA.

On the following interesting

SUBJECTS.

I. Of the Origin and Design of Government in general, with concise Remarks on the English Constitution.

II. Of Monarchy and Hereditary Succession.

III. Thoughts on the present State of American Affairs.

IV. Of the present Ability of America, with some miscellaneous Reflections.

Written by an ENGLISHMAN.

By Thomas Paine

Man knows no Master save creating HEAVEN,
Or those whom choice and common good ordain.
THOMSON.

PHILADELPHIA, Printed

And Sold by R. BELL, in Third-Street, 1776.

In order to make *Common Sense* accessible to all Americans, Thomas Paine did away with philosophical language and wrote in a simple style that included Biblical references.

"*It is not enough that human rights should be written in the books of philosophers and in the hearts of virtuous men; it is necessary that ignorant or weak men should read them in the example of a great people. America has given us this example. The act which declares its independence is a simple and sublime exposition of those rights so sacred and so long forgotten.*"

MARQUIS DE CONDORCET, French philosopher, 1786

and that all political connection between them and the State of Great Britain, is and ought to be totally dissolved." Seven of the colonies supported the resolution; the other six (New York, New Jersey, Pennsylvania, Delaware, Maryland, and South Carolina) weren't yet ready to do so. When no agreement could be reached after two days of debate, the Congress decided to delay the final vote on Lee's resolution for three weeks, until July 2. In the meantime, the delegates could contact their colonial governments for instructions on how to vote.

"May it be to the world, what I believe it will be, (to some parts sooner, to others later, but finally to all,) the signal of arousing men to burst the chains, under which monkish [self-denying] ignorance and superstition had persuaded them to bind themselves, and to assume the blessings and security of self government."

THOMAS JEFFERSON, author of the Declaration of Independence, June 24, 1826

25

Although the vote on independence had been delayed, the Congress appointed a committee to draft a declaration explaining to the world the colonies' justification for breaking free of Britain—they wanted to be ready if the vote came back in favor of independence. John Adams, Benjamin Franklin, Thomas Jefferson, Roger Sherman of Connecticut, and Robert Livingston of New York were assigned to the committee. After meeting briefly to discuss the document's format, the committee asked Jefferson to write the first draft. The quiet, 33-year-old lawyer, who had a reputation as a gifted writer, accepted the task.

Entrusted with drafting the Declaration of Independence were Benjamin Franklin, Thomas Jefferson, Robert Livingston, John Adams, and Roger Sherman (pictured left to right).

For the next several days, Jefferson rose every morning before dawn and headed for the parlor of the two-room suite he had rented in a house on the outskirts of Philadelphia. With a portable writing desk on his knees, he dipped his goose quill pen in ink and began to write. As he worked, Jefferson thought about the ideas of Enlightenment thinkers such as Paine and English philosopher John Locke, who had stated that government should be formed by the consent of the people. Jefferson also recalled much of what he and fellow Virginian George Mason had written for Virginia's new constitution only weeks earlier.

With these thoughts in mind, Jefferson wrote and rewrote, crossing out words here and adding new phrases there, until he was satisfied. When he was done, Jefferson had composed a five-part declaration of independence.

After writing the Declaration of Independence, Thomas Jefferson remained active in U.S. politics. He served as governor of Virginia, American ambassador to France, secretary of state, and vice president, before being elected president in 1800. During his presidency, Jefferson greatly enlarged the territory of the U.S. through the Louisiana Purchase, which extended America's borders to the Rocky Mountains. Even with all of his achievements, Jefferson was proud of his work on the declaration to his dying day. He wanted to be remembered as "author of the Declaration of American Independence, of the Statute of Virginia for religious freedom, and Father of the University of Virginia."

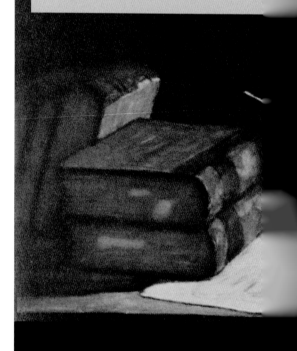

A Declaration by the Representatives of the UNITED STATES OF AMERICA, in General Congress assembled.

When in the course of human events it becomes necessary for one people to dissolve the political bands which have connected them with another, and to ~~assume among the powers of the earth the~~ assume among the powers of the earth the separate and equal station to which the laws of nature & of nature's god entitle them. a decent respect to the opinions of mankind requires that they should declare the causes which impel them to ~~the~~ the separation.

We hold these truths to be self-evident; ~~sacred & undeniable;~~ that all men are created equal ~~& independent,~~ that ~~from that equal creation they derive~~ they are endowed by their creator with ~~rights~~ ~~equal~~ inherent & inalienable rights; that among ~~which~~ these are the ~~preservation of~~ life, & liberty, & the pursuit of happiness; that to secure these ~~ends~~ rights, go-- vernments are instituted among men, deriving their just powers from the consent of the governed: that whenever any form of government ~~shall~~ becomes destructive of these ends, it is the right of the people to alter or to abolish it, & to institute new government, laying it's foundation on such principles & organising it's powers in such form, as to them shall seem most likely to effect their safety & happiness. prudence indeed will dictate that governments long established should not be changed for light & transient causes: and accordingly all experience hath shewn that mankind are more disposed to suffer while evils are sufferable, than to right themselves by abolishing the forms to which they are accustomed. but when a long train of abuses & usurpations [begun at a distinguished period, &] pursuing invariably the same object, evinces a design to ~~subject~~ reduce them † under absolute Despotism, it is their right, it is their duty. to throw off such government & to provide new guards for their future security. such has been the patient sufferance of these colonies; & such is now the necessity which constrains them to [expunge] alter their former systems of government. the history of ~~his~~ the present king of Great Britain is a history of [unremitting] repeated injuries and usurpations, [among which appears no solitary fact ~~to contradict the uniform tenor of the rest but all have~~] all of which have in direct object the establishment of an absolute tyranny over these states. to prove this, let facts be submitted to a candid world [for the truth of which we pledge a faith yet unsullied by falsehood]

H. Franklin's handwriting
mr. Adams's handwriting

The introduction to the declaration stated why the colonies had written it: to explain "the causes which [impelled] them" to separate from Britain. The next part, the preamble, stated that "all men are created equal" and have certain "inalienable" (later changed to "unalienable") rights, including, "Life, Liberty, and the pursuit of Happiness." It also asserted that when governments abuse their power, the people have the right to rebel. Jefferson then listed 27 grievances against King George III, among them that he had repeatedly dissolved representative houses in the colonies and imposed taxes on the colonists without their consent. After describing the ways in which the colonists had attempted to peacefully resolve these issues, Jefferson concluded by renouncing all allegiance to the British throne.

"No other American document has been read so often or listened to by so many weary and perspiring audiences. Yet, despite interminable repetition, those well-worn phrases have never lost their potency and charm."

DUMAS MALONE, Thomas Jefferson biographer, 1948

29

After completing his draft, Jefferson showed it to the committee, which made minor changes before submitting it to the Congress on June 28. Before the Congress could review the declaration, however, the delegates first had to vote for independence. On July 1, the day appointed for their votes to be cast, the delegates again debated the issue. After nine hours of debate, a poll revealed that only nine colonies were in favor of independence. Although this was a majority, the Congress wanted such a momentous decision—one that would require the complete unity of the colonies—to be unanimous.

Edward Rutledge of South Carolina proposed that the official vote be postponed until the next day, hoping that some of the colonial delegations might change their votes overnight. By July 2, South Carolina and Pennsylvania had agreed to vote for independence. In addition, Caesar Rodney, an absent delegate from Delaware, had arrived to swing his delegation in favor of independence. When the colonies finally registered their votes that day, 12 said "aye" to independence. The delegates from New York abstained; although they personally supported independence, they had to wait for instructions from their colonial legislature before casting their vote. (They were finally instructed to vote in favor of independence two weeks later.)

Now the Congress could turn its attention to Jefferson's declaration. As Jefferson squirmed nervously at the back of the room, the Congress pored over the 1,817-word document line by line. The delegates made almost 100 changes and cut the document by about a quarter before approving it on July 4. Immediately, copies of the declaration were made and sent to all the colonies, where it was proclaimed in public squares, prompting the outbreak of spontaneous celebrations.

"I was determined to see how they all looked as they signed what might be their death warrants. I placed myself beside the secretary, Charles Thomson, and eyed each closely as he affixed his name to the document. Undaunted resolution was displayed on every countenance."

WILLIAM ELLERY, Rhode Island delegate to the Second Continental Congress, on the signing of the Declaration of Independence, August 2, 1776

30

Although Thomas Jefferson listened quietly as the Congress edited his draft of the declaration beginning on July 2, 1776, he was not happy with the "mutilations" made to the document. Despite the fact that Jefferson himself owned slaves, he was especially upset over the removal of a long section condemning slavery. The replacement of his conclusion with Richard Henry Lee's original resolution for independence also frustrated Jefferson. The author of the declaration was so convinced that his draft was superior to the Congress's that he included the text of his "fair" copy in his autobiography and also gave copies to several friends.

Before drafting the Declaration of Independence in 1776, the Second Continental Congress had voted in 1775 to create the Continental Army, made up of colonial militias.

The resolution for American independence might never have passed if not for Delaware delegate Caesar Rodney's effort to get to Philadelphia in time to vote. Rodney was in Delaware helping to suppress loyalist activity when a message from fellow delegate Thomas McKean arrived, saying that a vote on independence was imminent. Knowing that without him, his state's delegation would be deadlocked—with McKean in favor of independence and the other delegate, George Read, opposed—Rodney set out on horseback for the 90-mile (145 km) journey to Philadelphia. Riding all night through fierce storms, he arrived just in time for the beginning of the fateful meeting.

This painting by artist John Trumbull captures the historic moment when Congressional delegates signed the American declaration, committing the colonies to revolution.

As the declaration continued to be cheered throughout the colonies, an official copy, handwritten on parchment, was being prepared by Timothy Matlack, a Pennsylvania calligrapher. When the copy was ready, the Congress again gathered, and on August 2, 1776, all of the congressional delegates present signed their names to the document (only John Hancock had signed it on July 4). They left space for those who could not be present to add their names later (for a total of 56 signers). As the members of the Congress added their signatures one by one, they knew they were committing treason against the Crown; if captured by the British, they could be hanged. They also knew that they were committing their states to a war with the most powerful empire on Earth. Only if they won that war would the declaration they had so painstakingly adopted mean anything.

34

Copies of America's Declaration of Independence quickly made it across the Atlantic Ocean to England, where the government refused to legitimize the document by commenting on it directly. The Crown did, however, commission a lawyer named John Lind to write the 100-page "Answer to the Declaration of the American Congress." This document offered a point-by-point denial of the American colonists' claims.

Meanwhile, the war for independence continued in the American colonies, where the fighting was concentrated in New York, New Jersey, and Pennsylvania. Throughout the war, the colonial army found itself greatly outnumbered by the British, who had more than 30,000 well-trained soldiers on American soil. In contrast, Washington had about 20,000 untrained men, and only about 5,000 of them were available at any given time, as most were unwilling to enlist in the Continental Army for more than a few months. Although small state militias often assisted the Army, they were usually inexperienced and unorganized. Yet the colonists fought with passion to protect their homes and families. Relying on the element of surprise, Washington's forces attacked and retreated time after time, spreading confusion and inflicting casualties on the British forces.

In October 1777, American troops forced the surrender of 5,800 redcoats at Saratoga, New York. Afterward, Britain made an offer to the colonists: they could return to their former status as British

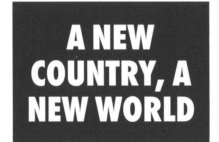

A NEW COUNTRY, A NEW WORLD

The battle at Saratoga, New York, which resulted in the surrender of nearly 6,000 British troops, emboldened American soldiers and began to turn the tide in the colonies' favor.

"[Britain] will unite as one man, and teach this rebellious people, that it is one thing for them to say, the connection, which bound them to us, is dissolved, *another* to dissolve *it; that* to accomplish *their* independence *is not quite so easy as to declare it:* that there is no peace with them, but with the peace of the King: no war with them, but that war, which offended justice wages against criminals.—*We too, I hope, shall . . . [make] whatever efforts may be necessary, to bring this ungrateful and rebellious people back to that allegiance they have . . . so daringly renounced.*"

JEREMY BENTHAM, British philosopher, "Short Review of the Declaration," 1776

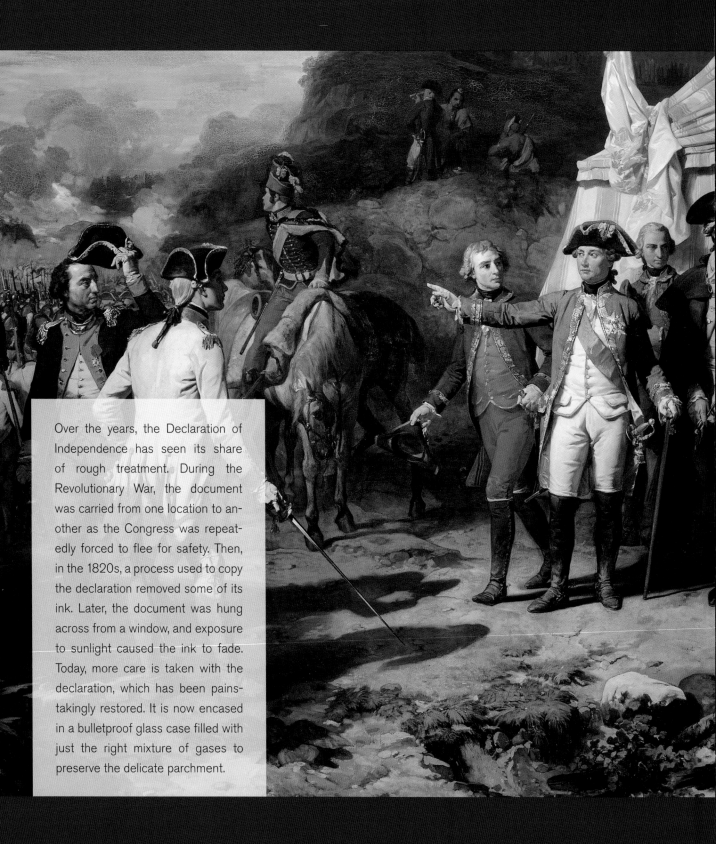

Over the years, the Declaration of Independence has seen its share of rough treatment. During the Revolutionary War, the document was carried from one location to another as the Congress was repeatedly forced to flee for safety. Then, in the 1820s, a process used to copy the declaration removed some of its ink. Later, the document was hung across from a window, and exposure to sunlight caused the ink to fade. Today, more care is taken with the declaration, which has been painstakingly restored. It is now encased in a bulletproof glass case filled with just the right mixture of gases to preserve the delicate parchment.

The Seige of Yorktown was a death blow to Britain's hopes of holding power over the colonies; when the redcoats surrendered on October 19, 1781, the war's end was in sight.

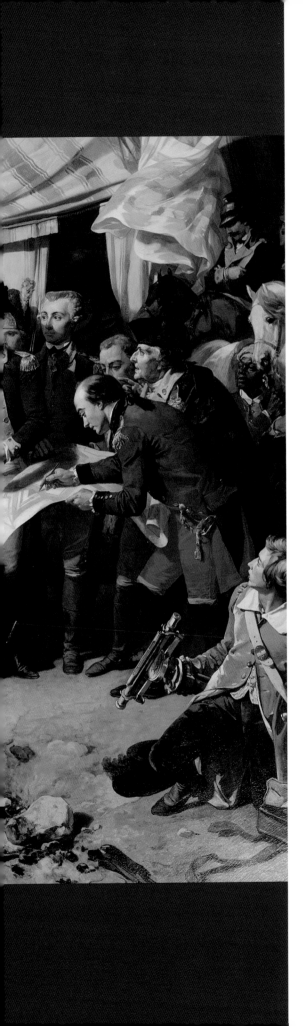

colonists, and Parliament would no longer have the power to tax them. The Americans, now determined to win their independence, refused. Soon after, France agreed to send troops to the colonies; Spain and Holland also became American allies.

Even with these new allies, American victory was still not assured. By June 1780, the American situation looked bleak, as the British had moved south and captured Savannah, Georgia, and Charleston, South Carolina. In late September 1781, however, French and American troops laid siege to the city of Yorktown, Virginia, where British soldiers were stationed. As French ships blocked escape by sea, American and French troops on land barraged the redcoats with artillery fire. Finally, after 20 days, on October 19, 1781, Britain surrendered, bringing major fighting to an end. Two years of peace negotiations followed before the Treaty of Paris (named after the French city in which the negotiations were held) was finally signed, making American sovereignty official.

America was free, but the war had taken a toll on the new country. More than 27,000 Americans had died from wounds or disease during the more than six years of fighting. In addition, civilians had been assaulted and killed, and many homes and farms had been looted or burned to the ground. Among them were the homes of 12 of the men who had signed the Declaration of Independence. (Five other signers had been captured by the British during the course of the war, and nine signers died before the fighting came to an end.)

Although the physical damage to America was on its way to being repaired soon after the war's end, a new, more serious threat arose: dissension. By 1783, the 13 states of the new nation hardly lived up to their new name, as they were barely united. Ruled by the Articles of Confederation, which served as the country's first constitution, the U.S. was a very loose association in which each state acted almost as a separate country. Although the Congress had the authority to make war, enter into alliances, and coin money, the states held on to the power to levy taxes and manage trade. Because of this, the Congress had little means of raising

"I am not sorry that the line of conduct seems chalked out. The New England Governments are in a state of rebellion [and] blows must decide if they are to be subject to this Country or independent."

KING GEORGE III OF BRITAIN, 1774

38

without Difficulty and without requiring
any Compensation.

Article 10th

The solemn Ratifications of the
present Treaty expedited in good & due
Form shall be exchanged between the
contracting Parties in the Space of
Six Months or sooner if possible to be
computed from the Day of the Signature
of the present Treaty. In Witness
whereof we the undersigned their Ministers
Plenipotentiary have in their Name
and in Virtue of our Full Powers signed
with our Hands the present Definitive
Treaty, and caused the Seals of our Arms
to be affix'd thereto.

Done at Paris, this third Day of September, In
the Year of our Lord one thousand seven hundred & Eighty three.

D Hartley   John Adams
             B Franklin   John Jay

In the last line of the Declaration of Independence, the signers pledged their "lives," "fortunes," and "sacred honor" in support of the declaration. These were not idle words. The 56 men who signed the document knew that if they were captured, the punishment would be severe. Only a year before, rebels against British rule in Ireland had been hanged, then taken down and disemboweled while still alive, then beheaded. Despite such knowledge, the signers all wrote with a steady hand, except for Stephen Hopkins of Rhode Island, whose hand shook from palsy. Yet even he declared, "My hand trembles, but my heart does not."

funds to carry out its work or repay its war debts to foreign nations such as France and to soldiers who had served in the Revolution. The states also began to bicker over trade agreements. Under such a system, the now-retired George Washington began to fear that the country was "fast verging to anarchy and confusion."

As a result, 55 leaders representing every state except Rhode Island gathered in the State House in Philadelphia once again in May 1787, this time to create a new governing document. Under the leadership of Washington, who had been called out of retirement, delegates to the Constitutional Convention first had to decide how the states' power would be divided: Would each state get one vote, as had been the case in the Continental Congresses, or would the states be assigned a specific number of representatives based on their population? Ultimately, the Convention established a bicameral legislature composed of two bodies: the Senate and the House of Representatives. Each state would have an equal number of representatives in the Senate. The number of legislators a state sent to the House of Representatives would be determined by its population (the larger the state, the more representatives).

In addition to establishing the form of the legislature, the Constitution also set up the executive branch (the presidency) and the judicial branch (the courts) of the government and separated the powers of federal and state officials. When the Constitution was approved by the Convention on September 17, 1787, it became the first written constitution of any major country. Two years later, Washington was chosen to serve as president in the nation's first-ever presidential election. At the urging of Washington and other leaders, the Bill of Rights was added to the Constitution in 1791, guaranteeing Americans basic rights, such as freedom of worship, speech, and assembly.

"A great revolution has happened—a revolution made, not by chopping and changing of power in any one of the existing states, but by the appearance of a new state, of a new species, in a new part of the globe. It has made as great a change in all the relations, and balances, and gravitation of power, as the appearance of a new planet would in the system of the solar world."

EDMUND BURKE, British philosopher and statesman, 1780s

Even as the new country's government was being set up, thousands of people across the Atlantic who had heard about America's freedom set out for the U.S., seeking a new life away from the tyrannical rulers of Europe and Asia. Others decided to stay in their own countries and follow the American example

42

George Washington stood among the greatest early Americans; when he died in 1799, cavalry officer Henry Lee said that he was "first in war, first in peace, and first in the hearts of his countrymen."

of fighting for freedom in their homeland. In July 1789, revolutionaries
in France—tired of the corruption
and waste of the Crown—stormed a
Paris prison called the Bastille, spark-
ing the French Revolution. The next
month, the new National Constituent
Assembly introduced the Declaration
of the Rights of Man and of the Citi-
zen. Inspired in part by the American
Declaration of Independence, the
French document proclaimed that
"men are born and remain free and
equal in rights," including the rights
to "liberty, property, safety, and resis-
tance to oppression."

Soon, the French and American
Revolutions were inspiring more revolutionary movements across the globe.
By 1826, more than 20 countries
in Europe, South America, and the
Caribbean had issued their own decla-
rations of independence. At the beginning of the 21st century, more than

America's founding fathers turned to a form of government called democracy, meaning "rule by the people," for their new country. In a democracy, citizens either vote on laws themselves (called direct democracy), or they elect representatives who vote for them (called representative democracy). Since its founding, the U.S. has been a representative democracy, in which the people of each state elect government officials to carry out their will. Although democracy was first practiced in ancient Greece and was also present to a degree in England (where the king's power was limited by an elected parliament), the U.S. was the world's first modern democracy.

As America began to find its way as a sovereign country, the French people launched their own bid for freedom when Parisians stormed and captured the Bastille royal prison.

"*I have often inquired of myself what great principle or idea it was that kept this Confederacy so long together. It was not the mere matter of the separation of the Colonies from the motherland; but that sentiment in the Declaration of Independence which gave liberty, not alone to the people of this country, but, I hope, to the world, for all future time. It was that which gave promise that in due time the weight would be lifted from the shoulders of all men. This is a sentiment embodied in the Declaration of Independence.*"

U.S. PRESIDENT
ABRAHAM LINCOLN,
February 22, 1861

President Abraham Lincoln

half the countries of the world had similar documents, many of them adopted in part from the American declaration.

In addition to inspiring revolutions in other parts of the world, the Declaration of Independence provided the spark for a number of movements closer to home. In 1808, the U.S., inspired in part by the declaration's ideal of equality for all men, outlawed the importation of slaves. Five decades later, President Abraham Lincoln called on the words of the preamble to the declaration in his quest to completely abolish slavery in America. The declaration also served as a foundation for the women's rights movement, which issued the Declaration of Sentiments in 1848, asserting that "all men and women are created equal."

Today, the preamble is the best-known portion of the Declaration of Independence, which is now housed at the National Archives in Washington, D.C. Every day, some 5,000 people look upon the document that changed the course of history by establishing what would come to be the most powerful nation on Earth. Even those Americans who don't travel to see the declaration in person commemorate it every year on July 4, the anniversary of the day it was adopted. With fireworks, parades, and backyard barbecues, people across the country celebrate a fact that has become a taken-for-granted part of their everyday lives but was once revolutionary: the U.S. is "and of right ought to be, free and independent."

47

The freedom fought for and attained some 230 years ago is celebrated every summer with waving flags and fireworks displays on the Fourth of July, America's Independence Day.

BIBLIOGRAPHY

Armitage, David. *The Declaration of Independence: A Global History*. Cambridge, Mass.: Harvard University Press, 2007.

Baldwin, Leland, and Robert Kelley. *Survey of American History*. 2nd ed. New York: American Book Company, 1967.

Cooke, Donald. *Our Nation's Great Heritage: The Story of the Declaration of Independence and the Constitution*. Maplewood, N.J.: Hammond, 1972.

Driver, Stephanie Schwartz. *The Declaration of Independence*. Hauppauge, N.Y.: Barron's, 2004.

Gragg, Rod. *The Declaration of Independence: The Story behind America's Founding Document and the Men Who Created It*. Nashville, Tenn.: Rutledge Hill, 2005.

Hawke, David Freeman. *Honorable Treason: The Declaration of Independence and the Men Who Signed It*. New York: Viking, 1976.

Kallen, Stuart, ed. *The 1700s: Headlines in History*. San Diego, Calif.: Greenhaven, 2001.

INDEX